UNDER THE FORTUNE PALMS

UNDER THE FORTUNE PALMS
TOM CLARK
TURKEY PRESS 1982

For Shelley
All best

[signature]
April 19, 1984
Santa Barbara

CONTENTS

"Here if anywhere else in America,
I seem to hear the coming footsteps
of the Muses."

W. B. YEATS

Those who came from places
that produced corn, wheat, butter & eggs
to a place that produces celluloid images, computer chips,
drive-in taco stands & aerospace components
have never stopped wondering, "What am
I doing here?" They believe some destiny awaits the place.
They believe this because somebody told them so.
It's a belief that's really a lot more like a feeling.
They can't remember who it was that sold them
all those neon poems
you hear echoing through this cathedral of empty
headed intentions they call home. The only false
note here is my referring to them as "they."

2

TROUBLE IN PARADISE

I didn't come here to
milk your sacred cow
or even to
slaughter her

As a matter of fact
the first time
I looked at her crosswise
she turned into goat cheese

They say this part of California
Is paradise on earth for the roof rat,
Who loves the palms & vines of the middle classes,
The ubiquitous fruits, the delectable nuts & ivy.

Just another genus struggling to become indigenous,
When it arrives they switch the menus. But it won't leave.*

----

* cf. the medfly

4

Those bungalows of San Roque
so perfect yet oddly sad
("a little wood & stucco
to keep the sun out")
always remind me of
where the Nelson family lived
way back in the days of Hi Oz
Hi Pop Hi Rick Hi David.

Everybody in that family was Okay
every day for a whole decade.
And when Ricky turned out to be
a low rider, it was still okay.
And that's the way it is today
among the petticoat palms
of Calle Noguera
and Puesta del Sol.

You can't rain on the parade
of the petit bourgeois
because it doesn't have one.

They say San Roque
is only one step
away from heaven

but keep in mind
that could be a
step in the wrong direction

6

SHORT BATS

Everybody here is good at what they do
Which is, in most cases, Nothing

Cecil Rhodes
wd. have liked it here
excellent climate
plenty of nat. resources
high prop. value
& natives nearly as totally subdued
(&/or supine)
as their favorite catchphrase indicates

8

This scene evokes (if anything)
viet nam, where the body
count was all that showed
whereas here, the body
show is all that counts

JANE FONDA HAS A SCRAWNY ASS

I've been in the lower class and the middle class
those two were enough for me and that's why
I don't want to join the exercise class

10

Play beach volleyball
Make surfboards & live at Dana Pt.
Pick up chicks galore
Shine it on & get a good suntan
Catch cancer from the chemicals in the water
Die a grotesque death
Have a movie made about your life
Make sure you look thin in every scene

THE CLASS DOESN'T STRUGGLE ANYMORE

Why is it so unsurprising that
the little man in the white coat
who drives the small motorized cart
across the manicured putting green
that grows like crushed money
between the bungalows of the Biltmore
doesn't appear to enjoy the acquaintance
of the thin old man in the italian sweater
who emerges from one of the bungalows
tugged along by a tiny expensive dog?

12

The lost hard "g" in Los Angeles
a consonantal position swept away like all else
in the great laissez faire flood
from Chula Vista to Los Olivos
Jack Webb said it as
"Los Ang-less"

So did my grandfather, who liked it here

Nowadays though, they say it soft
without much meaning
to change it, but changing it
all the same—like taking the "o"
out of "Adios," and putting it back in "Idiot"

Or like the big developer in tartan plaids
who says to the local don of Zoning
Bon giorno! on a beautiful morning
before they divvy up the rights to the aqua
for another patch of the sun-deluged townhouses
that stretch from here to Solvang
in an unraveling irregular torus like an orange
peeled by an unsteady celestial hand

Nothing but psychodrama
& disillusionment
in the canyons of the wealthy

Still there's a swell sunrise
up Gibraltar Road a ways
where the red-yellow spectra
of the rising sun to the left (east)
get up above the marine layer
down around Ventura County
and all Montecito's
hazed terrarial shadows erupt at once

The resultant sky is a story
of wild peach liqueur
spilled on dirty pillows

SOUTH COAST FLORA

In the face of all these
exotic introductions
like all forms of the petticoat palm
with its little white flowers on top
shaped like dollar signs
the native coastal shrub & chaparral
is made to Stand Back
as is anything native anywhere
in the swirling movement or onslaught
of small arrested dunes
of floating capital

The meaning of objects in
the desert is great
but here, where everything
is grown-over
with human clusters
nothing is clear
everything is shifting,
constructed
& merely apparent

THE PACK APPROACHES THE MISSION

The sun dies into pink smog off Goleta
& over toward Point Conception
the violet reptiles of the night
begin to slide across the sky
like pieces of neon tubing.
In such lighting the wild dogs
are held momentarily at bay.

The building blocks of a superior logic
seem to slip into place
with a quiet authority. The moon comes up.
There is a small click. It is evening.

It is of course the
evening of the very rich
who do not like to lean
into the wind. They stand, the pair
beyond the camphor tree on Laguna Street
bathing in its fragrance. Two old dames.
Perhaps they are not very rich after all.
It may be just the blue hair that fooled me.

It may have been the failing light.
It may have been the falling rose-colored
flowers of the pink flame tree,
or pieces of their pods,
which are covered with rusty wool,
that fell through the air
and affected my vision.

It may have been the pollen in the air,
the fluffy cotton heads which have
just burst from the floss-silk trees,
or floating strands of the dark
hair-like fibers that are
shed by the fortune palms
whenever the breeze arises.

There is a serenity about this apparition
but it is abruptly broken
by the peremptory bark of the pack-leader,
who, poised at the brink of the trees, signals
with a crazed snarl for the rest of the pack to advance.

18

DEAR DOCTOR

a rat swam toward me
in my hot tub

I shut my eyes
and took my b.p.
by bio-feedback

& outside I heard
the random snarling
of the packs

There are people so sick
in Lynwood, Downey,
Paramount & Hawthorne
as to leave out
paper plates of food
in alleys
to keep the wild dogs alive.

UNDER THE FORTUNE PALMS

Some people think meanings are hard to find
In the 1980's decade of great emptiness
Among the bungalows of Samarkand
I stood under the fortune palms
And watched for a sign to blow by
In the throbbing Santa Ana
But all that came my way
Was the remote echo of a woman's voice
From down around Xanadu Street
Calling for her dog to stay

Suddenly on the Mission lawn
A guy tosses a frisbee catching sun glints
Into the vermillion jaws of dusk
While above the frayed palms
A great sherry party takes place in the western sky
With catering by Giambattista Tiepolo
Eternity is in that moment
As if the sun were going down over Venice
—and there one stood, *maestro di pintore*,
Calculating the finishing touches—
Instead of only off Goleta

'HALLOWEEN ON THE SOUTH COAST'

Halloween on the south coast
red bugles break into
ceruleans & manganese blues
the white blossoms of the yucca
pasted against absolute cobalt
the salmon pink of the Santa Ynez
deep palm greens & straw ochres
cobweb grays of the pines
the silver dollar turnover
of eucalyptus in the slipstream
northeast wind chases the aerosols
off & brings in all these colors

Wild form, deep form, form out of the
                                Arabic night
God, your conspicuous discrete
desert stars are trucks of light
on very distant highway 101's
                                over which
I am hitchhiking tonight
The waves feathering out in ink
beyond Obispo, toward Conception
toward Surf, a black like blue

O I want to say it was on Betelgeuse
or Vega   on a night blue like
this that I first met you
                                how I felt
when contacted by your hot Adriatic
A man who caters ice
sculptures to barbecues
in Death Valley
might know something about this

24

You were wearing your arrival suit that day
It was a sight to turn one's head up to the sky
Where the Crab bingled to center for one station
It seemed like the beginning of a raging time
Light spread like a butter patty across the mesas
While the sun rose like a heated metal coil
Flung-up with skill by a starboard flinger
Into a wall of such brightly reflecting rocks
That their face, tilted to the West, received
The sun of afternoon in phases of altering
Color so deep it went into the roots of Hue.
This being true, why didn't we linger? You so wise,
Reminded me we hadn't yet arrived.

Qualifying by my powerlessness for a life
of following the air currents that blow down
the corridors of the Labyrinth of Lost Angles
which are like the sub-grandstand on the other
side of the walk-through mirror in *Orphée*
I find that midway through the whole journey
my fatalistic noir ethos disappears & is
replaced by a sense of being a dull weak guy
impecuniously pumping gas for a living
on a lonely high desert where no cars pass
I was given a long term contract on this job
The kind where they don't pay any royalties
There's nothing to do but watch the rats
run around the pump in the dawn's pink oxymorons

26

WINNING THE KEWPIE DOLL MADE OF PLATINUM,
I SLIP ON THE MIRROR BRINGING IT HOME TO YOU

The elegance of the 2-bit hustler
who pulled off a dangerous caper
keeping a rendezvous with Dr. Snuff
all to win a silver star
with which to decorate the night sky—
his whole collection pasted there
on the ceiling
of the cold bedroom of his lover—
is very probably spurious
Nevertheless the struggle toward freedom—
O fallen angel of the moon
whose passions fill my notebook
of foolish behaviors—
is one I will act out forever

WHY WE NEED A NEW BALLAD MODE

What's simple
joy division
in the beginning
later makes
every little cell
wring its hands
and bang its head
against the bulkheads
of its being

that's why love
can't be trusted

28

The tracks of the cricket
carve a groove
the knife's voice
thick heat
else a whisper of bituminous
in the dying rocks
like hunting opals
this quest of love
through arid rivers
of dried up lightning

So it's a desperate exile cold desert light that flees
The salmon pink of the Santa Ynez at 5:52 AM in November
Color with power to make men forget slow exile days
Knowledge w/o power to move, light moves in no trees
Men stand around dying in the deserted Sierra Madre
What else is there to do? Horses die too, also camels
Overcome by quiet of Egypt, the sense of inspissate gloom
All this air, all these clouds
That go down with Moses into a cadmium
Dawn exploding in soaring stages over the bullrushes

30

Over the Santa Barbara Racquet Club
Like a gold tennis ball dandled on a gas jet
The sun bounces up into the sky.

On those courts the most beautiful women
In the world rub eau de cologne into their round legs
And then leap like springboks at passing shots,
Gulping-in vitamins of light out of the burning blue.

They get up this early to play because of fires from within.
They give their utmost up and on.
The fires smolder.
The story is always old and always new.
If I tell it to you here, it is only because it is what
They have said first with their bodies,

Bodies which may burst into flame at any moment.

I stand
on my pedals
racing down Foothill above
     the Tennis Club

Where there is no
  caring
      there is no feeling
        —but then
from the deep crevasse below me
  there arises
a broken emotional cry
  "Forty-love!"

32

LITTLE ELEGY FOR BOB MARLEY (d. 5/11/81)

I turn the bike home thru the freeway haze at Rincon
Heading west into the flow of the commuter pack
It's hard to concentrate thru this fog of mistrust
This aerosol inflected loss of perspective
It's probably meant to serve as a relief from history
But history still has a way of stating its case
As when the evil snail wraps itself around the sad faced
Singer-saint's spinal stem & wrings out the last of his existence

The frightening ballast of dust licks
The sky that fades from lavender to beige
The red tips of the bougainvillea are
Lit by some kind of internal gas
Also legible on maps of purgatory

An unfolding topology of tracks
Over which
Cars move between the flat dark areas
Through the
Motionless light diffusing haze

Quit your gripes about the bad air
being the dead end
of civilization as known

According to *Rédiffusion du Sud*
it's only a serious case
of dissolution by aerosols
in *Le Cimetière Tropique*
where invisible particles corrode
the anti-frontiers
and leak a desert music
into the marine band

An advancing state
(in other words)
of post-Club Med tristesse
expressed thru the business end
of a Porsche exhaust pipe

for Dennis Cooper

If you've got a problem, come on over
It's like heaven up here
but you can get lost in the likeness
fumbling in a wet similitude through
too many consecutive turquoise days
tiptoeing around the corrals of the rich
leading up to the brink of the autopsy
sometimes it almost makes you wish
you hadn't died, so you couldn't dig all this

don't be tempted to suppose
those very retired germans
with the big money market accounts
and the agape stares
in the supermercado
are of no account
they're all characters in
the santa barbara book of the dead
and as they pass beneath
the classical queen palms
in their big detroit motors
one must contribute some act
of reverence, even if it's only
reaching down (in one's imagination of korps)
& picking up some dog shit
(easy to find)
& flinging it at them

WHAT'S THE DIFFERENCE BETWEEN
AN AVOCADO & A RARE BOOK?

There may not be many things
I can join with the land in saying
But there's this much
After my visit to Short Bats
I know how it feels
To have been farmed

38

The palm trees   the bars
     in my internalized sing
               sing
A peon feeling meaningful
   he's missing something

We are not fools
    or terrorists
  we are stooges

This is a movement
    not a weakness of character

I will be a stooge in
    order to survive
  the coming pulsations of Class.

Even my resilience is limited

The crashing silence of the palm trees

The rubber ball is on its
Eight thousandth bounce
The logic of elasticity
Is growing blurred

It is 5:19 AM

I have a feeling
Like being X-rayed
In the privacy of my house

You see us as ridiculous and you laugh
We don't care if you laugh
We'd laugh too

We are a miscellaneous class
Our backgrounds are diverse
The things we do are various
But here is what unites us
We only act this way for cash

We are Stooges Anonymous
We lower ourselves for money
You may humiliate us
You may embarrass us
You may do anything
You want to us
Because we are
Stooges Anonymous!

We're educated but we got no ideas
No standards No beliefs No class
Speaking strictly we're trash
Speaking any way at all
We're still trash
Got no manners No personalities
We're stooges
Stooges Anonymous
We do it for cash

We lower ourselves for money
We do any kind of act
You may think we're pathetic
You're right we say
Just don't try telling us
The check's in the mail

42

A POLYESTER NOTION

We have reached the other side of the harbor
the sails of the yachts are slapped against the sky
like acrylic colors straight out of the tube
equally thoughtless and simple is the deep
lavender backdrop against which the ochre
mountains are flatly & theatrically stacked

We can keep on continuing along this line
as far as the grave of Ronald Colman or we
can double back and visit Ross MacDonald's
locker at the swim club though I seriously doubt
Robert Mitchum will be there what with
the polo season opening this week & all that

Twist away the gates of steel
DEVO

O wide blossom-splashed private drives
Along which sullen mouthed little guys
In motorized surreys
Ride shotgun over spectacular philodendra!
O paradise of zombies!
O terminal antipathy to twist
And shout!
O hotel sized garages
Inside which smoothly tooled imported motors
Purr like big pussies under long polished hoods!
O fair haven of killjoys
United to keep surfers off
One of the great beach breaks
Of the West Coast!
O floral porticos, flowers
Of de Kooning, de Chirico
Chateaux!   Estates where jokes
Aren't funny!   What secret meaning awaits
Behind your stone & steel gates
Your walls of bougainvillea
Your date palm lined roads
Your quiet oak shaded lake
Like a European protectorate in Tanganyika?
Surely nothing disorderly, nothing disarrayed
Nothing at all except the great Pacific swell

Of money!

44

A pointed tin roof
cute wood shingles
stuffed macaws
revolving ceiling fans
banana trees
birds of paradise
pineapple daiquiris
bamboo swizzle sticks
sarongs soaked in lizard spit
sigh
I'm starting to think
maybe Tiki's too tacky
even for me

ELECTION DAY IN SLEEPY MISSION

Life should have enough arresting moments
to create at least a tropism in Xanadu

but little is expected by those who
live in the environs of the lawn bowling court

for them it is a perennial Mondo Samarkanda
and Reagan now coming home to roost

in their sunset is like the great snork bird
of Papua homing in on orange juice

46

IN A VACUUM, A SINGLE EMISSION CAN BECOME SMOG

This part of the country is definitely a
corner pocket when it comes to word
music. For instance although he's
got a tin ear over there under the palm
trees and Nazi architecture of Cal Tech
the only poet/editor in SoCal who can fit
an entire cantaloupe in his mouth
without opening his lips
is being interviewed by the L. A. Times
as a force in the Arts
because of his new magazine named after farts
featuring the works of Mr. Dull and Mr. Slack,
snores in front and snoozes in the back.

The L. A. Times makes sure
to get all this straight so tomorrow
morning out there under the rat cluttered palm trees
of Nowhere, the suckers & hustlers & dilettantes
can lap it up. And when they do,
it will thereby become The Culture.

Art rusts away in the constant
depreciation of commerce
Funny that should occur to me now
Funny it should be by stumbling
into such a reputedly sunny zone
that one should find
this anti-Atlantis of the soul
the Valley of the Shadows
known by its sign, a chill blankness
deep in the red pumping engine

Here in the capital of insincerity
where even the clouds tell lies
and even the palms are inauthentic
the Museum of the Immortals'
outdoor sculpture garden
is populated by casts of the famous
for whom
it's certainly too late to flee

If it's true their memory's forever stained
a dull copper green by the
incrustation of profit, a residue
tarnishing their names, then too
it's equally true the rules of the game —
i.e. the conditions of oxidation —
were written
that way from the very start.

48

THE MUSES' EXODUS

Out of the fading morning fog, in a powdery blue day
under the bays of the oak and the laurel
one can almost imagine the soft forms moving

to a hype that insinuates like music from a zither
deep there, out of the rocks, by the spring
where the oracle waits with lips pressed
almost as tight as the drawer of the cashbox

The quest for winter sunshine washes
The gasping survivor up on the shore
Much that's done isn't meant
Much that's meant isn't done
I take it up & at the beck & call
Of some remote agency I stick it in
& when it's over I pull it out again
Like the bloody *assegai* of a born liar
Every wave lines up behind the last one
The days wash away the days
The waves wash away the shore

THE NEW THING I TOLD MYSELF ON OLIVE STREET

yesterday was another one
of the last days left on earth
but who's counting this string
of pearls? who'd want to
those my thoughts as I hobbled
trying out my homemade shoes again
in the new valley of dolls down
canon perdido street way
where in this gray a.m.
the men are already lined up
outside the state assistance office
with (at this late date)
not even the appearance of
false cheerfulness left
So I make it around the corner
there's a guy lying face up
to the sky on city sidewalk
wino I guess with bottle
in paper bag only out like
a light or some dead amigo
on slab in city morgue
"Don't be afraid" I told
myself afterward limping
away "to go down
deep and blow upwards
from there, to the Lord,
like a diver in shit ocean..."
talking to myself these days...

"Reach down
        to your toes and know
and know
how deep it goes..."
                kinda humming it
"down past the pink notes
to where they get blue
outa squids"... I crossed Carrillo...
"nobody down there know your name
nobody down there know you
and you know the real sound
you get (that moan)
is the one you pull out of
looking up at the bottom
all the time, anyhow besides"

but it didn't help

52

Twenty-one guns
and a snorkel
won't get you through heaven's
gates of coral
I mean you can
swim out as deep as you like
toot your salute
with no matter how many
sweet & graceful notes
into the breeze marine

Here come the dark fins
cutting across the water

The young sharks feed peaceably in the shallow waters.
Because they are strong and proud, they get a chance
                                         to be silly.
The old sharks move out to the deeps, hungry, restless
                                         and driven.

They are only serious.

54

"Apply another time?
Are you trying to be
the Kenneth Patchen
of your generation?"

That was my wife
implying
I ought to give up

Kenneth Patchen
                never gave up
and that's how I want to be
obnoxious, aggressive
out of it but at least not
part of the twilight
of the idiots

piety requires us to honor truth
above our friends
but if we have none of the latter
it makes the whole thing easier

56

The fact that when they dug up Windsor Way
after the calamity, he was still sitting
there, was considered much less
remarkable than the fact that anyone
could have expected to find something different

The tunnel is the eye of a needle.
The light at the end of the tunnel is
caused by the miniature railroad
train of the future bearing down on
us with incredible fission. Casey
Jones is clutching the throttle with
a skeletal hand. Hot cinders
spark and sizzle his nose hairs.
Ahead lie the killing labors of the
the Modoc Grade. But Casey
Jones is not afraid. His foot
is attached to the dead man's pedal
by bandages of destiny. Nothing
can halt this continually arriving train
nor widen its rapidly narrowing
gauge. Casey fires up his Camel and rides.

5⁸

Those men whom the gods wish
to destroy, they first make
mad, and then, when the first white flecks
of foam speckle the men's lips—the spit
of bewilderment, of overpowering visions—the gods
throw their heads back and they
laugh and laugh, they laugh and they
laugh, until they are rolling on the floor
of the heavenly TV lounge

POEM FOR JACK KEROUAC IN CALIFORNIA

You hear that dead man
rave and blow, down under
the ground, where form
gets wild and it's like Steve
Carlton plunging his arms into
buckets of uncooked rice
and working his fingers around
to get the power up
through his muscles into the
tendons of his neck and
shoulders and what have you
the bigger the digger
the deeper the grave

60

Plip by plip
strict dribbles of wasted smoop
accumulate into trickles
that wet the beaks of parched tributaries only slightly
Bud Powell died in 1966
with a cigarette still hanging from his lips
and from that point on
the long, coruscating lines that leap and dart with dry lunacy
have been hard to find

THE RETIREMENT OF SUPERMAN

Shivering once and
wrapping my red and blue cloak tightly around myself
I traveled to a rare and terraced land
where there were trees of alabaster
in forests of blasted gold
under petrochemical dawns
I goofed and dreamed, life was very great
human beings didn't need me any more
I received a monthly stipend of 720 free hours
whenever I got hungry all I had to do
was drop my head down
into the submarine dollar ferns of heaven
and chew

62

PSEUDO-MEDITERRANEAN

Time passes like a funeral
you're taking the cure
the yucca flower
reaches up to the sun
like a white candle
melts into the blue
& becomes invisible

Life is made to burn
death is like the sun
life among the mirages
it's the only one

Because it won't accept my no any more
I'll ray out into the day
But I won't say the sayless sentences
The boats will sail into the soft
White spray making their way out
Past the drill rigs' spidery struts
To the blank horizon becoming gray-
On-white dots like aces of snow
Fading away into Pacific February
Out there where the current pulls
Beneath the flat cold slate blue
Voicing a certain I don't know what
That down deep has so strong a draw
Nothing lost to it ever surfaces
Before I fall I'll look below
I'll know what I have to know
It'll be a knowledge like the hole in a donut

COLOPHON

175 copies were printed by Sandra Liddell Reese
on a Vandercook 219. The type is Goudy Modern,
hand set by Harry Reese. The paper is Frankfurt
white. On 26 copies, lettered A to Z, an original
acrylic on canvas painting by Tom Clark wraps
around the book. All of the books have been hard
bound at Turkey Press, Isla Vista.